A HISTORY OF BRITAIN

Acknowledgments:
The author and publishers would like to acknowledge the use
of additional illustrative material as follows:
Page 37: Aerofilms Ltd; pages 16, 40 (top left and centre right):
Bodleian Library, Oxford; page 24: Janet and Colin Bord;
cover and pages 19, 51 (top): Britain on View (BTA/ETB);
pages 40 (bottom left), 49 (top), 50: British Library;
page 25: The Syndics of Cambridge University Library;
page 28: The Cathedral Shop, Canterbury;
page 15: by courtesy of the Rt. Hon. Viscount de l'Isle, VC, KG;
cover and page 23 (top): Essex County Council (photographer – Peter Rogers);
page 13 (bottom): Robert Harding Picture Library;
page 23 (bottom): S. G. Harrison; page 43 (2): The Mansell Collection;
drawings on pages 7, 42 (centre right): Anne Matthews;
pages 13 (top), 21: Museum of London;
page 33: Royal Armouries Board of Trustees;
page 12: Royal Commission on the Historical Monuments of England;
cover photographs (2) and pages 27, 31 (bottom).
by courtesy of His Grace the Duke of Rutland CBE;
page 32 and endpaper decoration: Warwick Castle.
Designed by Chris Reed.

Ladybird books are widely available, but in case of
difficulty may be ordered by post or telephone from:

Ladybird Books – Cash Sales Department
Littlegate Road Paignton Devon TQ3 3BE
Telephone 0803 554761

A catalogue record for this book is available
from the British Library

Published by Ladybird Books Ltd Loughborough Leicestershire UK
Ladybird Books Inc Auburn Maine 04210 USA

Contents

The Middle Ages

by TIM WOOD
illustrations by JOHN DILLOW

Series Consultants: School of History
University of Bristol

Ladybird

The Middle Ages

This book covers a period of over two hundred years, from 1272 – 1485, a time known as the **Late Middle Ages**, or **Late Medieval Period**. It was a time of violence and wars, as kings struggled to control the powerful *barons*, and the barons fought one another for more land. The wars often brought death, famine and plague to the troubled countryside.

The Middle Ages – time chart

Date	Kings and people	What happened
1250		
	Edward I 1272-1307	Conquest of Wales. War in Scotland
1300		
	Edward II 1307-1327 Robert the Bruce	Uprising in Scotland. Robert is proclaimed King of Scotland. Wins Battle of Bannockburn 1314
	Edward III 1327-1377	Hundred Years' War began between England and France 1337
	Black Prince (Edward III's eldest son)	Battle of Crécy 1346
		Black Death plague 1348. Growth of the wool trade
1350		Chaucer b.1345 d.1400.
	Richard II 1377-1399 (Grandson of Edward III, son of the Black Prince)	Wrote *THE CANTERBURY TALES* in the 1380s
	Wat Tyler John Ball	Peasants' Revolt 1381
	John Wyclif	First complete translation of Bible into English 1382
	Henry IV 1399-1413 (Cousin of Richard II. Forced Richard to give up the throne)	Barons grew powerful

Date	Kings and people	What happened

1400 — War with France. Battle of Agincourt 1415

Henry V 1413-1422
(Son of Henry IV)

Henry VI 1422-1461
(Son of Henry V)
Joan of Arc

Henry marries Margaret of Anjou 1445

1450 — Hundred Years' War ends 1453. Loss of French lands

Wars of the Roses begins 1455, between the Lancastrians (Henry VI) and the Yorkists (Richard, Duke of York)

Edward IV 1461-1483
(Cousin of Henry VI) — Triumph of the Yorkists

England's first printed book 1477 — printed by William Caxton. Produced nearly 100 titles up to his death in 1491

Edward V 1483
(Son of Edward IV)

Richard III 1483-1485
(Uncle of Edward V) — Battle of Bosworth 1485. Last Plantagenet, Richard III, died. The throne passed to the House of Tudor

People at the beginning of the Middle Ages

Most of the people living at this time were very poor. The real power lay in the hands of the king and a few very powerful landowners.

EDWARD II
murdered

THE KING: During the Middle Ages ten different kings ruled England with the help of the barons. If a king was weak, the barons turned against him and tried to seize power themselves. Four kings were murdered and three came to the throne by violence.

RICHARD II
murdered

The most successful kings were usually the best fighters. They could control the barons, and so were able to raise enough money to run the kingdom well.

EDWARD III
by violence

HENRY VI
murdered

HENRY IV
by violence

EDWARD V
murdered

RICHARD III
by violence

THOSE WHO FOUGHT: The barons owned huge areas of land. They built castles to protect their lands and many had their own soldiers.

THOSE WHO PRAYED: Religion was very important to medieval people, so everyone went to church sometimes several times a week. There were many large monasteries, where monks spent their lives working and praying.

During the Middle Ages, the church became rich and powerful. Church leaders were often advisers to the king and many monasteries became rich through the wool trade.

THOSE WHO WORKED: Most ordinary people were peasants or serfs. They had to live and work on land owned by the rich barons.

A drawing based on a medieval manuscript showing peasants at work

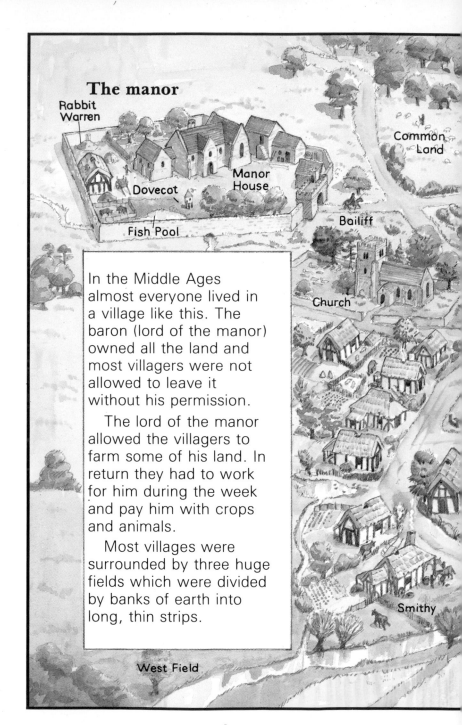

The manor

Rabbit Warren

Common Land

Dovecot

Manor House

Fish Pool

Bailiff

Church

In the Middle Ages almost everyone lived in a village like this. The baron (lord of the manor) owned all the land and most villagers were not allowed to leave it without his permission.

The lord of the manor allowed the villagers to farm some of his land. In return they had to work for him during the week and pay him with crops and animals.

Most villages were surrounded by three huge fields which were divided by banks of earth into long, thin strips.

Smithy

West Field

Forest

Each villager farmed some strips in each field, so the good and bad land was shared out fairly.

A lord probably owned several manors. He visited each in turn, taking his family, servants and most of his possessions with him. When the lord was away, the *bailiff* was left in charge.

North Field

Mill

Mill Pond

Common Land

lord of the manor

Villagers gathered wood, berries and nuts from the forest, and grazed their animals on the *common land*, which they shared. They had everything they needed except salt and iron, which they had to buy from the nearest town

South Field

Working on the land

Every year the *reeve* and the villagers decided what to grow. One field was used as a pasture for animals. The second was sown with wheat (for bread) and the third with barley (for beer).

All the villagers helped, including the children. Most of the work was done by hand, although there were oxen to help to pull heavy loads or to plough.

The reeve was elected by the villagers, or appointed by the bailiff. He shared out the jobs in the village

Sickles were used to cut the wheat

The mill, where grain was ground into flour

Barns for storing grain

Flails were used for threshing, to separate the stalks from the grain

Winnowing: the wind separated the grain from the stalks

11

The peasant's house

Peasants lived in wooden huts with roofs made of thatch. The family lived in one end, animals in the other. The huts were dirty, smelly and dark.

'Wattle' was woven twigs. 'Daub' was mud plaster

A medieval house, probably belonging to quite a wealthy family, at Didbrook, Gloucestershire. The frame was made of large wooden beams. The spaces between the beams were filled with wattle and daub

Loft where the children slept

dung heap

ox stalls

rushes on floor

The main food for a peasant family was bread. Some peasants kept chickens, pigs and cows, for eggs, bacon and milk. Water was not clean, so often people drank beer. During a long winter many peasants went hungry and some starved.

Pottage, a thick soup, was sometimes made from beans, vegetables and herbs, perhaps with a scrap of meat thrown in. It was cooked in a *skillet*, which stood in the hot ashes

Smoke-hole plastered round with clay

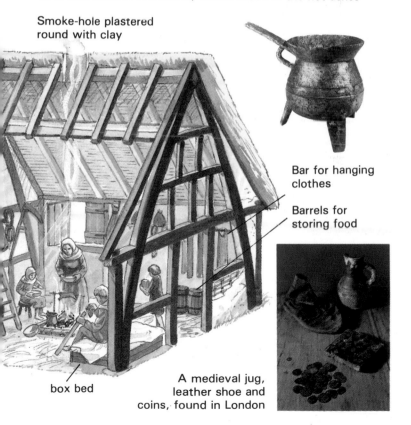

Bar for hanging clothes

Barrels for storing food

box bed

A medieval jug, leather shoe and coins, found in London

catching rabbits

Food

stag hunting

The lord of the manor ate fresh food all year round. He kept doves and tame rabbits. He could hunt wild boar or stags in the forest, or go hawking. Peasants were not allowed to hunt, and any caught doing so could be punished or even hanged.

hooded falcon

Falcons were trained to catch wild birds. Hoods kept them quiet while they sat on their owners' wrists

Menu

Meal	Lords	Peasants
6am Breakfast	White bread 3-4 meat courses.	Dark bread, ale.
11am Dinner	Up to 12 dishes Meat, fish, wine,	Bread, cheese, ale.
6pm Supper	Pies, cakes, meat.	Pottage, ale.
9pm Livery	Cakes, tarts, spiced wine.	

The Great Hall, Penshurst Place, the biggest medieval hall in England. It was heated by an open fire in the middle of the floor and food was served through the doors which led to the kitchens behind the wooden screen

A banquet

On feast days the lord of the manor held a banquet in the Great Hall of his manor house or castle. It could last up to five hours with as many as forty different dishes.

Minstrels sang and played in a gallery. Jesters, acrobats and tumblers entertained the feasters

The *butler* brought in the wine

Guests ate off *trenchers*

This picture, taken from a medieval manuscript, shows servants boiling food in cauldrons and roasting meat on a spit

The lord of the manor and his special guests sat at the high table

coat of arms

The *marshal* led the procession from the kitchen

A young *noble* carved the meat

The *almoner* carried a dish to collect money for the poor

The chief cook carried his badge of office — a wooden spoon

Salt dish. Rich people sat 'above' the salt, poor people 'below'

Going on a journey

In the Middle Ages, although most people never left their villages, some people had to travel.

Roads were just tracks, muddy in winter and very dusty in summer. People travelled in large groups for protection against outlaws.

Inns were usually dirty and overcrowded

Pilgrims travelled to shrines, while government officials and nobles travelled on the king's business. A few peasants went to market, merchants travelled about buying and selling goods, and soldiers went off to war.

Carriages were not very comfortable, so rich people often travelled on horseback. Ox carts were slow, so merchants mostly carried their goods on packhorses.

Travelling chest, belonging to King Henry V

Heavy loads like corn or building stone were sent by river in boats. For longer journeys, such loads were sent by sea.

Wool being loaded onto a ship, to be sent abroad

Towns

Almost fifty seven million people live in Britain today. In the Middle Ages, the population was much smaller (three to six million). Towns, though they grew in importance during the Middle Ages, were small. The largest city was London. In the year 1300, only 60,000 people lived in the city, compared with about seven million today.

Fire was a great danger in the towns, where wooden houses and workshops were crammed close together. People threw their rubbish straight out of the windows so the narrow streets were dirty, smelly and often swarming with rats and flies.

Shops had workshops behind them where craftsmen worked. Streets were named after the shops in them, such as Leather Lane or Bread Street. Many towns still use these street names.

medieval shoes

shoemaker

The guilds

Guilds were clubs started by the most skilled of all the workers, the master craftsmen. Each trade had its own guild and only guild members were allowed to make and sell those goods in the town.

Becoming a master craftsman

Parents paid the master craftsmen to train their children as *apprentices*. An apprentice slept in the workshop and was paid nothing.

He could not go to inns or get married. If he did not work hard, he was beaten. After seven years' training he became a *journeyman* and received his first pay.

Several years later the journeyman produced a *masterpiece* as a guild test. If it was good enough, he was taken into the guild and allowed to have his own shop.

A masterpiece

Thaxted guildhall

WHAT THE GUILDS DID:

1. made sure that members did not work too many hours or charged too little;
2. gave money to members who were old or sick;
3. checked and tested that goods were well made;
4. made sure that members were not cheated.

At festivals, guilds put on plays from the Bible, like this one, still performed in Chester.

Fairs

Fairs were held once a year in certain places, such as Boston in Lincolnshire and Winchester in Hampshire, and lasted several days. Merchants came from all over Europe bringing silks from China, wine from France, furs from Russia and weapons from Spain. People came long distances to dance, hear news, and watch clowns, jugglers and performing animals.

stalls

Poor people bought tools, pots, pans, ribbons and cheap ornaments

Cheats were put in the *stocks* (see right) or *pillory*

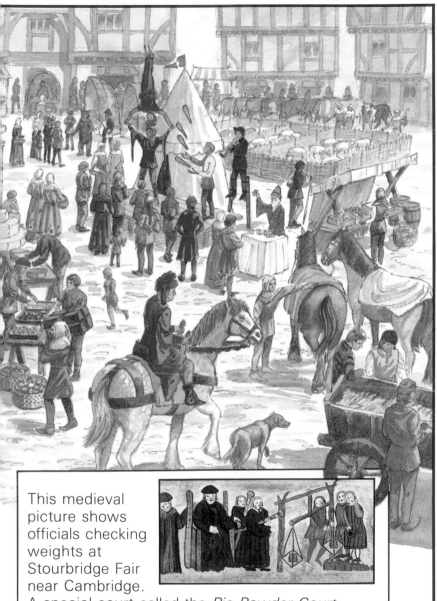

This medieval
picture shows
officials checking
weights at
Stourbridge Fair
near Cambridge.
A special court called the *Pie Powder Court*
sorted out any arguments on the spot.

Monasteries

In the Middle Ages, monks and nuns spent their lives cut off from the rest of the world in monasteries or nunneries. Although they spent most of their time praying, many also farmed the land round the monasteries to feed themselves. They gave food and money to the needy, allowed travellers to stay free for two nights and ran hospitals for the poor.

Key
1 church
2 farmland
3 kitchens
4 library
5 guesthouse
6 brewery
7 bakehouse
8 dormitory
9 hospital
10 Abbot's house
11 washrooms and toilets
12 refectory (dining room)
13 almonry (where the poor came for food)

Dole cupboards, like this one, were found at monasteries. Inside there would be bread and drink for the poor

2

13

1

7

8

9

6

Pilgrims

In the Middle Ages people who had done something wrong and wanted to be

forgiven often went on a pilgrimage to pray at a shrine.

Some pilgrims went abroad to places like Assisi

Shrines are holy places, such as holy wells or the tombs of saints.
Canterbury and St Albans were popular shrines to visit. Here is an artist's drawing of pilgrims at Thomas Becket's tomb. Today a plaque marks the spot where the Archbishop was murdered in Canterbury Cathedral in 1170

MEDIEVAL PILGRIMS

knight

nun

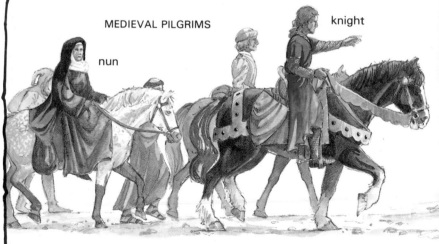

or Rome in Italy, or even as far as
Jerusalem in the Holy Land. The journey
was very exciting and sometimes
dangerous, with strange places to visit
and new people to meet. A pilgrimage
was the only chance
for rich and poor
people to meet as
equals.

Stalls and shops sold food
and drink. Pilgrims bought
relics or souvenirs such as
holy water, pieces of saints'
clothing and special badges

merchant

peasant

Sick people also went on pilgrimages
hoping for miraculous cures at the shrine

Sport

Medieval people played many of the sports we play today, but the games were often more violent.

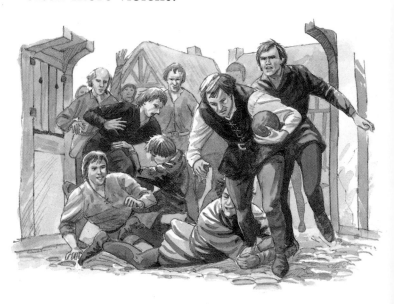

Football was played between all the men of two villages. The ball was a pig's bladder stuffed with peas, and the aim of the game was to carry it across the fields and place it on the market cross of the other village.

There were no rules, so players were often hurt and sometimes even killed. King Edward III banned the game because he thought that people were more interested in playing football than in practising their archery.

The most popular sports involved animals fighting and were often very cruel

cock fighting

Bear baiting – a chained bear was attacked by dogs

Many sports were just fighting, like wrestling and shin kicking

quarter staffs

archery

skittles

stoolball

Knights

Knights were landowners who had been given land as a reward for fighting for the king or baron. Each knight used his own horse and weapons and could be asked to spend up to forty days each year serving in the king's army.

crest

chain mail

helmet

visor

haute piece

pauldron

breastplate

battleaxe

gauntlet

shield

cuisse

poleyn

sword

greave

sabaton

mace

A boy from a wealthy family trained for up to ten years to become a knight, by serving first as a page and then as a squire. As a squire, he looked after the knight's armour and helped him to dress for battle. He learned how to ride and how to fight.

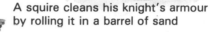

A squire cleans his knight's armour by rolling it in a barrel of sand

Prince Edward, Edward III's eldest son, won his spurs to become a knight at the Battle of Crécy. He was sixteen years old and became known as the Black Prince because of the colour of his jousting armour. Here, he wears the arms of England (lions) and France (lilies). His head is resting on his great helmet which bears his lion crest.

Tournaments

Tournaments were held so that knights could practise the art of fighting. Knights came from near and far to test their skills by *jousting* with one another. Crowds of people came to watch.

Each knight was allowed three lances. When three had been broken, the fight continued on foot. A defeated knight gave up his horse and armour

A wooden fence called a tilt kept the knights apart

Heralds announced the contestants and trumpeters gave the signal to charge. Each knight tried to knock the other off his horse. The fight continued on foot until one knight was beaten. Although they fought with blunted weapons, knights were often injured or killed.

Today some people believe that knights had to be hoisted onto their saddles. This actually never happened

In battle, each knight wore his own badge or coat of arms so that people knew who he was

Castles

Kings and barons built castles to protect their lands. After defeating the Welsh, Edward I of England built many castles in Wales to control the country. Other castles were built in the north of England as protection against Scottish raiders.

The increasing use of gunpowder and cannon meant that, after 1350, fewer castles were built.

1 LADDER

2 MANTLET: Protective screen let archers move closer to the walls

3 BATTERING RAM

4 BELFRY: Movable tower covered in wet animal hides to make it harder to burn

5 HOARDING: Overhanging gallery gave cover for defenders

Caerphilly Castle, Glamorgan was begun in 1271. It was surrounded by several moats, artificial lakes and a screen wall 305 m (1000 ft) long

6 MINE: Tunnel dug under wall, filled with wood and then set on fire to make wall collapse

7 MANGONEL: Twisted ropes provide the power for this catapult to hurl stones

8 ARROW SLITS: Specially shaped to give defenders good view and to give attackers very small target

9 HOT PITCH, OIL, WATER or SAND (which got into an attacker's armour and made him itch) were poured down

The Hundred Years' War

During the Middle Ages, parts of France were ruled by the English and parts by the French. Each side wanted the land owned by the other. The war which broke out between them in 1337 lasted until 1453 and is known as the Hundred Years' War.

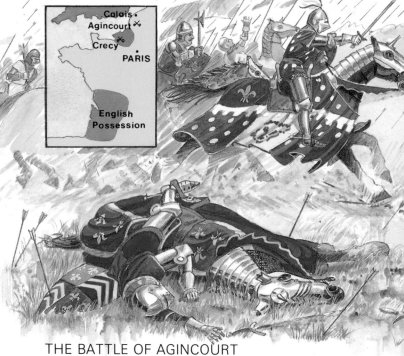

THE BATTLE OF AGINCOURT
The battle took place on 25th October 1415.
The French had high hopes of winning.
Reports said they had 50,000 men whilst the English, led by Henry V, had only 6,000.

The French had chosen the site carefully but as their first line of attack charged, they were caught in a field of mud caused by rain the night before.

It was the skill of the archers that won the battle. Their steel-tipped arrows could kill an armoured knight at two hundred paces. A skilled archer could fire twelve arrows a minute. The battle lasted for nearly three hours. Although the English won this great battle and others, they could not win the war.

Men-at-arms with long *pikes* defended the archers, who were protected by a line of stakes

The longbow was made of yew wood and the arrows were made of ash

Medicine

People in the Middle Ages did not live as long as people do today. Most died before the age of fifty. Doctors were not allowed to cut up dead people to find out what caused disease, so they knew little about curing sickness.

Doctors believed that illness was often caused by 'badness' in the blood. Sometimes they would cut a vein to let some of this 'bad' blood out.

Physicians used astrological charts, herbs, spells and charms as cures. Some prepared ointments made from animal fat, blood or dung. Most of their cures were useless.

Surgeons were barbers who also pulled out teeth and did small operations. Their shops had red and white striped poles outside to show the blood and bandages of their trade.

bleeding bowl and knife

Worms called leeches were used to suck out blood

A page from a book of herbal cures

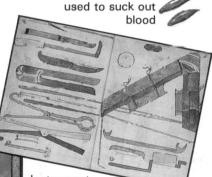

Instruments used in operations

A manuscript from the 13th century showing a medieval brain operation. *Anaesthetics* were unknown, so this patient would have suffered terrible pain and probably died soon after

The Black Death

In 1348, a terrible plague reached
England. It came from China, carried by
the fleas which lived on black rats.
People bitten by these fleas developed
lumps as big as apples in their armpits,
followed by the red and black spots
which gave the disease its name, the
Black Death.

Black rats lived in the holds of ships and carried the plague
from China

The plague
flea,
magnified
many times

Doctors did not understand what caused
the Black Death, and there was no cure.
Within two years the plague had killed
one-third of the population.

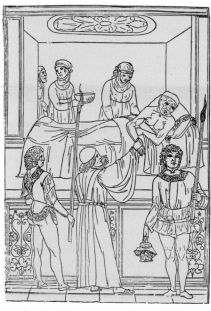

Doctors wore outfits like this to protect themselves. The beak was stuffed with herbs to filter the air

A physician, attending a Black Death patient, holds a scented pomander to his nose

The dead were collected on carts and buried together in large graves

THE PEASANTS' REVOLT

1 After the Black Death there were fewer
   peasants to farm the land. The overworked
   survivors grew to hate their manor duties.

   The peasants wanted to be paid wages and
   to be free to leave the manor. They were
   angry when a law was passed to stop this.

2 In 1381, King Richard II brought in a poll
   tax to pay for the war against France.
   Everyone over the age of fifteen, rich or
   poor, had to pay one shilling (5p), a large
   sum of money in those days.

3   The peasants attacked their lords. In 1381, John Ball, a poor priest, encouraged the men of Kent to march to London to try to get higher wages and their freedom.

Young King Richard, who was only fourteen at the time, met the peasants. Their leader, Wat Tyler, was killed by the Lord Mayor of London.

4   The king promised to help, but when the peasants returned home, their leaders were hanged. No more poll taxes were introduced and in time wages began to rise.

What people wore

Poor people wore cheap, rough, woollen clothes. Rich people wore finer woollen clothes decorated with fur and jewellery.

1300-1400

PEASANT

LADY

NOBLEMAN

hooded cloak

loose tunic

clogs

loose surcoat

surcoat lined with fur

undergown

People wore wooden clogs to keep their feet out of the mud

Shoes were made of thick cloth, leather or velvet

Fashions for wealthy people changed a great deal during the Middle Ages. Towards the end of the period people were richer, so they bought better clothes with more decoration such as embroidery and fur trimmings. Women's hats and hairstyles became very grand. Townspeople copied the styles of the rich, but they used cheaper materials.

1400-1485

MERCHANT

LADY

YOUNG MAN

head-dress

padded jacket or jupon

high collar

loose gown

thick, woolly tights

jagged sleeves

long robe

silk underskirt

Shoes became very long and pointed

People at the end of the Middle Ages

The Middle Ages, which came to an end in 1485, were times of great change.

THE KING: During the period, most kings had problems in ruling the country because of challenges by rich and powerful barons. Only Edward I, Edward III, Henry V and Edward IV were really successful in controlling them.

EDWARD IV

THOSE WHO FOUGHT: By 1485, which marked the end of the Wars of the Roses, the barons owned huge areas of England and many had become powerful, with large armies.

By the age of 21, Richard Neville, Earl of Warwick was one of the richest men in England. He was the most powerful baron in the country and had his own private army.

He supported his cousin, the Yorkist King Edward IV, during the Wars of the Roses. But his downfall came when he changed sides for the Lancastrians. He was killed at the Battle of Barnet in 1471

RICHARD NEVILLE

THOSE WHO PRAYED: By 1485, people no longer thought monasteries were important. Travelling preachers, called friars, were very popular and gave practical help to villagers.

People criticised the monks for being greedy – as this picture of a monk drinking wine suggests

THOSE WHO WORKED: By 1485, the Black Death and other diseases meant that there were fewer peasants. The surviving peasants had fewer manor duties and most were paid wages. Towns had become more important because of the wool and cloth trade. This brought wealth to the merchants and to the free labourers, or artisans, who wove the wool and made other goods.

Lavenham guildhall was built by the powerful wool guild

ROMANS 700BC – AD383	SAXONS AND NORMANS 383 – 1272	MIDDLE AGES 1272 – 1485	TUDORS 1485 – 1603

1083 yrs ⟩ 889 yrs ⟩ 213 yrs ⟩ 118 yrs ⟩

TIMELINE GUIDE TO *A HISTORY OF BRITAIN*

How we know

The events in this book happened over five hundred years ago — so how do we know about them?

Historians use EVIDENCE, rather like detectives do, to piece a story together.

Some BOOKS describing medieval life have survived to this day. One of the best known medieval writers is Geoffrey Chaucer who wrote *The Canterbury Tales*, a long poem about a pilgrimage in which each traveller tells the story of his or her life.

Many books at the time were written by monks.

They decorated their work with small pictures, showing scenes from the lives of medieval people. How many original medieval pictures can you spot in this book?

The Shambles in York, one of the most famous medieval streets in Britain

Archaeologists have *excavated* medieval sites and there are many towns that have areas and buildings dating back to the Middle Ages. There is a list of places to visit on page 56.

OBJECTS found by archaeologists are often stored in museums. Most of the objects are made of metal or stone. We have fewer objects made from cloth or wood because they rot easily.

Some of these old objects seem strange to us. What do you think this is? You will find the answer on page 56

The legacy of the Middle Ages

The two most important things invented during the Middle Ages were guns and printing.

William Caxton did not print his first book in England until 1477. By 1485 most books were still written by hand and very expensive, but the invention of printing meant that new ideas could spread more easily.

The invention of guns slowly changed the way battles were fought. Castles could be easily battered down by cannon, so they became less useful.

SOME MEDIEVAL INVENTIONS

windmill

public clock

rudder

glass mirrors

compass

spinning wheel

spectacles

wheelbarrow

Glossary

almoner: official collector of money for the poor

anaesthetics: drugs used before an operation so that the patient feels no pain

apprentice: learner of a craft, being trained

archaeologist: someone who digs up and studies ancient remains

artisan: craftsman; person who works with their hands

bailiff: lord of the manor's chief officer

baron: a powerful noble

butler: servant in charge of wine and drink

common land: land on which all the villagers had the right to graze their animals

excavate: to dig up ancient remains

journeyman: a craftsman who had completed his apprenticeship and so could be paid a daily wage

jousting: combat between two knights, on horseback

marshal: servant in charge of ceremonies

masterpiece: finest piece of work

noble: person of high birth; from a good family

physician: medical healer

Pie Powder Court: a court held at fairs to punish thieves and cheats. The name probably comes from two French words, meaning 'dusty feet', referring to the travellers who came to the fairs

pike: long wooden stick with steel or iron head

pillory: wooden framework with holes for head and hands – used as punishment

reeve: a villager appointed by the bailiff or elected by the other villagers to organise their work

skillet: metal pot with feet, for cooking

stocks: wooden framework with holes for hands or feet for punishment

surgeon: medical person who performs operations

trencher: flat piece of wood used as a plate

winnowing: separating the wheat from the chaff

Index

Some places you can visit to find out more about the Middle Ages

CASTLES
Caerphilly Castle, Glamorgan
Harlech Castle, Gwynedd
Stokesay Castle, Shropshire
Tower of London
Warwick Castle, Warwick

FORTIFIED MANOR HOUSES
Markenfield Hall, North Yorkshire

HOUSES
Haddon Hall, Rowsley, Derbyshire
Little Moreton Hall, Cheshire
Penshurst Place, Kent

CHURCHES, CATHEDRALS, MONASTERIES
Canterbury Cathedral, Kent
Fountains Abbey, North Yorkshire
Rievaulx Abbey, North Yorkshire
Wells Cathedral, Somerset

TOWNS
Chester, Cheshire
Conwy, Clwyd
Lavenham, Suffolk
Ludlow, Shropshire
Newcastle upon Tyne, Tyne and Wear
York, Yorkshire

BATTLEFIELDS
Bosworth Field, Leicestershire
Bannockburn, Central Scotland

MUSEUMS
Weald and Downland Open Air Museum, West Sussex
Jewry Wall Museum, Leicestershire

The picture on page 51 shows a salting trough, used for preserving meat.